E
Cady Stanton

Founder of the Women's Rights Movement

Jeri Cipriano

Boston, Massachusetts
Chandler, Arizona
Glenview, Illinois
Upper Saddle River, New Jersey

Illustrations
2, 3, 5, 6, 8, 9 Luigi Galante.

Photographs
Every effort has been made to secure permission and provide appropriate credit for photographic material.
The publisher deeply regrets any omission and pledges to correct errors called to its attention in subsequent editions.

Unless otherwise acknowledged, all photographs are the property of Pearson Education, Inc.

Photo locators denoted as follows: Top (T), Center (C), Bottom (B), Left (L), Right (R), Background (Bkgd)

All Photos: Library of Congress.

ISBN-13: 978-0-328-67699-6
ISBN-10:   0-328-67699-3

2 3 4 5 6   V0FL 16 15 14 13 12

Growing Up

On November 12, 1815, a daughter was born to Margaret and Daniel Cady of Johnstown, New York. They named the baby Elizabeth. This girl was expected to grow up to be like other women of the time. She would not be allowed to vote or have a career. She would not even be allowed to own property.

But Elizabeth Cady did not grow up to accept ideas people had then about women. Instead, she became a fighter for women's rights.

What made Elizabeth Cady challenge the expectations people had about women? When she was 11 years old, her older brother died. Their father was overwhelmed with sadness. Later, Elizabeth Cady Stanton wrote that when she tried to comfort her father, Daniel Cady sighed, "Oh my daughter, I wish you were a boy."

The young daughter wanted to make her father feel better. "I will try to be all my brother was!" she told her father. And she did try. She learned how to ride horseback, and she did well in school. But her father was not comforted. He still wanted a son.

Daniel Cady was overcome with sadness at the death of his son.

At a young age, Elizabeth Cady realized that there were few opportunities available to her because she was a woman.

Women in the 1800s

Elizabeth Cady's father was a successful lawyer and judge. She enjoyed visiting his law office. She liked to listen in on the meetings he had. But what she learned in the meetings sometimes shocked her.

Young Cady learned that women had few rights under the law. Only men were allowed to ask a court for a divorce. Women could not earn their own money. Their children and their belongings were the property of their husband. And few jobs were open to them.

Elizabeth Cady found that being a girl limited her own opportunities. She had hoped to go to the same college her brother attended, but the college did not accept women.

Daniel Cady planned for her to go to a women's college. His daughter was not happy about the decision. She knew boys generally received a better education than girls did. Girls were just taught skills they would need to manage a house and care for children. Still, the college in Troy was better than most women's colleges. Cady did well, graduating at age 18.

In the Company of Abolitionists

After graduation, Cady lived the typical life of a wealthy young woman of that time. She visited friends and attended parties. Her favorite activity was going to Peterboro, New York, to stay with her cousin Libby Smith. Her cousin's father, Gerrit Smith, was an **abolitionist** who was working hard to end slavery.

Elizabeth Cady enjoyed being in the Smith home. There she could take part in conversations about serious topics, such as justice and slavery. Such conversations did not generally take place in the Cady home. Many of the people who visited the Smiths talked about the **emancipation**, or freeing, of enslaved people. Cady loved talking to people who wanted to make a difference in the world.

Elizabeth Cady's relative, Gerrit Smith, was a wealthy man who helped runaway slaves by selling portions of his land to them for just one dollar.

Cady visited the Smith home often during the 1830s. There, she learned how to speak her mind and stand up for her beliefs. One of the Smith's guests, a man named Henry Stanton, was impressed with Cady. Stanton, an abolitionist, was ten years older than Cady, who was 24 when they met.

Cady and Stanton liked each other and enjoyed being together. When Stanton proposed marriage, Cady said yes. Her parents, however, were against the idea. They believed that Stanton was too old for their daughter. In addition, because they did not agree with the abolitionists' position on slavery, they disapproved of Stanton's work as an abolitionist.

Cady did not know what to do. Then Stanton was invited to attend the World Anti-Slavery Convention in London, England. Cady did not want to be apart from him. She agreed to get married and decided to go with Stanton to England.

Marriage

Cady and Stanton were married on May 11, 1840. The wedding was not like other weddings of the time. Then, women promised to obey their husbands. Elizabeth Cady would not make that promise. She also decided that she would not replace her name with her husband's name and become Mrs. Henry Stanton. Instead, she added Stanton's name to her own, calling herself Elizabeth Cady Stanton. At the time, this was unusual.

Cady Stanton also shocked people when she did not address her husband in public as "Mr. Stanton," which was the practice back then. Instead, she called him by his first name, as married people did only in private.

Forming a Lasting Friendship

In London, Elizabeth Cady Stanton met other American representatives to the World Anti-Slavery Convention. One was a woman from Philadelphia, Lucretia Mott.

As Stanton and Mott walked around London together, they talked about more than slavery. Stanton was very happy to hear that Mott shared the same ideas she had about the rights of women. And she was impressed by Mott's intelligence and by how strongly she spoke about women's rights. Later, Stanton wrote that meeting Mott "opened to me a new world of thought."

Lucretia Mott, pictured here in 1842, was considered a "dangerous woman" by some people because she believed that everyone should have equal rights.

The Convention and Home Again

Though women were admitted to the World Anti-Slavery Convention, they were seated apart from the men. They were also told that they would not be allowed to speak. Stanton and Mott were outraged. They agreed then and there that one day they would have their own convention. It would be a convention for women's rights.

After the convention, the Stantons traveled for a while through Europe. But after six months, Elizabeth Cady Stanton was looking forward to seeing her family. Now that she was married, her father began to accept her husband. He invited the couple to live in the Cady home and even taught law to Henry Stanton.

After a year of living with her parents, Elizabeth and Henry Stanton moved to Boston, Massachusetts. Henry Stanton worked as a lawyer, and Elizabeth Cady Stanton became a mother. She gave birth to three boys between 1842 and 1845.

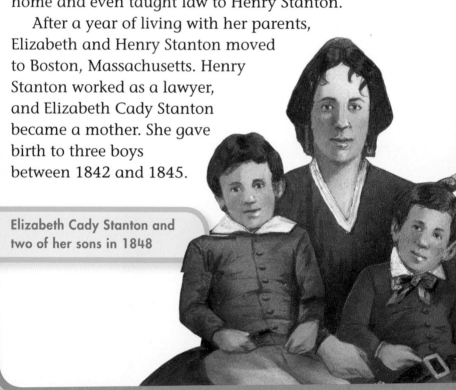

Elizabeth Cady Stanton and two of her sons in 1848

In the Declaration of Sentiments, Stanton wrote that "all men and women are created equal."

Seneca Falls, New York

In 1848, Elizabeth Cady Stanton received a letter from her friend Lucretia Mott. The Stanton family had by this time moved back to New York, to a town called Seneca Falls. Remembering their promise in London, Mott invited Stanton to a meeting with four other women.

The women Stanton met were involved in the anti-slavery **movement**. But they believed that the problems women faced deserved their attention. They decided to hold a women's rights convention on July 19–20, 1848. Stanton reserved a meeting room in Seneca Falls. Then she put an announcement in the local newspaper.

To prepare for the event, the group drew up a statement of women's rights they called a Declaration of Sentiments. It was based on the Declaration of Independence that our country's founders signed in 1776. In the Declaration of Sentiments, the women listed their complaints. These included being denied an equal education and having no right to seek divorce. Stanton made sure they included a demand for women's **suffrage**, or the right to vote.

The Women's Rights Convention

Both men and women attended the Women's Rights Convention. Even Frederick Douglass was one of the participants. Douglass was a well-known abolitionist who had been enslaved. At the convention, Lucretia Mott asked women in the audience to speak up and voice their opinions, even though it was not the custom at the time for women to do so.

Stanton read from the Declaration of Sentiments, and then she circulated it among the participants. In all, 68 women and 32 men signed the document to show that they supported the ideas in it.

Reaction to the Seneca Convention

News of the Seneca Convention spread. Soon, newspapers across the country printed articles that made fun of the convention and of what the women and men there were trying to do. Many of the Declaration signers felt embarrassed and asked to have their names removed—even Elizabeth Cady Stanton's sister! Frederick Douglass was one of the few people to publicly support the women in articles he wrote in his newspaper, *The North Star*.

Despite the criticisms, support for the declaration's ideas grew. **Petitions**, or written requests, for property rights and suffrage circulated. In 1850, women's rights conventions were held in several states. At each convention, Stanton was praised as a leader of the women's rights movement.

A New Style

One of the ideas in the women's rights movement was a call for more comfortable clothes. In the 1800s, women's dresses were made with up to 35 yards of fabric. They were so heavy and tight that some women had trouble breathing. Stanton's cousin, Libby Smith Miller, came up with a style of pants that women could wear. Amelia Bloomer called attention to the new style in a magazine she published. The pants became known as bloomers.

A Partnership with Susan B. Anthony

In 1851, Stanton met her lifelong friend and partner in the movement for women's rights, Susan B. Anthony. Anthony was a former schoolteacher who had also worked as an abolitionist. Three years later, the two women began working to change some New York state laws that restricted women's rights. Stanton had seven children and did not have the time that Anthony had to go to meetings. But Stanton was a good writer and wrote speeches that Anthony delivered before the New York **legislature**.

In 1860, Stanton and Anthony convinced the legislature to pass new laws. These laws gave married women the right to have their own money and allowed mothers to keep their children after a divorce.

Stanton (seated) wrote of her partnership with Susan B. Anthony: "I forged [made] the thunderbolts and she fired them."

In Her Own Words

Elizabeth Cady Stanton wrote speeches that called for every human being—male and female—to have the same rights. Stanton wrote, "No matter how much women prefer to lean, to be protected and supported, nor how much men desire to have them do so, they must make the voyage of life alone." Therefore, women needed a say in all things that related to them—now and in their future.

The National Woman Suffrage Association was founded in 1869.

The National Movement

Changes were happening. After the Civil War, the fourteenth and fifteenth amendments gave rights to African American men, including suffrage. But these rights continued to be kept from women. Stanton and Anthony thought this was unfair and continued working to change the laws.

In 1869, Stanton and Anthony decided to form an organization called the National Woman Suffrage Association (NWSA). The women also founded a women's rights newspaper called *The Revolution*. The newspaper's goal was to convince the public to support women's suffrage.

Elizabeth Cady Stanton in 1902

In 1872, Susan B. Anthony and 150 other women voted in the presidential election. Anthony and some of the others were arrested and found guilty of voting illegally. So Stanton and the NWSA proposed an **amendment**, or change, to the United States Constitution that would give women the right to vote. The amendment was introduced in the United States Congress in 1878 and each year after. But for 40 years, it did not get enough votes in Congress to move to the state governments for voting. Approval from the states was necessary for the amendment to become law.

Elizabeth Cady Stanton worked hard for women's suffrage, but she had other goals besides getting women the right to vote. She wanted to make life better for women everywhere. Throughout the 1870s, Stanton toured the country and gave speeches on women's rights. She also wrote many articles. Later, she worked on several books, including one with Susan B. Anthony about the movement they had started.

Stanton Leads the Way

Elizabeth Cady Stanton died on October 26, 1902. After her death, one of her daughters found a letter she had written to President Theodore Roosevelt. Stanton had never had a chance to mail it. In the letter, she urged the president to support women's suffrage.

Another 18 years went by before all women in the United States gained the right to vote. On August 18, 1920, the Nineteenth Amendment was passed. Finally, women had the right to vote in national elections.

On November 2, 1920, more than eight million women voted for the first time in American history. Elizabeth Cady Stanton began the fight for women's rights and suffrage in 1848. Seventy-two years passed before women could vote. Many more years went by before women enjoyed the same rights and opportunities as men. But Elizabeth Cady Stanton had led the way.

After Stanton's death, the women's rights movement was carried on by others, such as these women demanding suffrage in 1917.

Glossary

abolitionist a person who works to abolish, or end, slavery

amendment a change to the United States Constitution

emancipation freeing from slavery

legislature the branch of government that makes laws

movement a group of people working together to bring about some result

petition a formal written request, signed by a number of people

suffrage the right to vote in elections